WALKING
MONASTERY
WAY

WALKING MONASTERY WAY

CELEBRATING THE 75TH ANNIVERSARY
OF ST. PAUL'S MONASTERY

SISTERS OF ST. BENEDICT OF ST. PAUL'S MONASTERY

MILL CITY PRESS

Mill City Press, Inc.
2301 Lucien Way #415
Maitland, FL 32751
407.339.4217
www.millcitypress.net

The front cover depicts the beautiful stained-glass window by artist Michael Pilla, reminding us of our baptismal call to follow Christ, the first and basic call of each Christian.

Paperback ISBN-13: 978-1-6628-5893-2
Ebook ISBN-13: 978-1-6628-5894-9

Table of Contents

Pencil drawing by Virginia Matter, OSB.
For 75 years, the various ministries of the Sisters of St. Paul's
Monastery have been rooted in the Benedictine cross.

Welcome

Catherine Nehotte, OSB
Prioress of St. Paul's Monastery

I recall praying Psalm 90 many times over the course of my 35 years as a Benedictine: "Seventy is the sum of our years, or eighty if we are strong." Attributed to Moses, it is one of the psalms we pray at the Liturgy of the Hours as Benedictine women of St. Paul's Monastery. As we celebrate our 75th year in 2023, I am pleased to introduce this continuing and compelling story of St. Paul's Monastery.

Sister Carole Sweely shared the story of our first 50 years as an independent priory in St. Paul, Minnesota, celebrating our golden jubilee with the publication of *With Grateful Hearts the Past We Own* in 1998. When we were founded in 1948, Archbishop Byrne reminded us of the "many graces offered in abundance." The Spirit has certainly brought us new opportunities in our most recent 25 years, and graces have abounded. However, our mission remains the same:

> *We, the Sisters of St. Paul's Monastery, are a community who live Gospel values expressed in the Rule of St. Benedict. Through our monastic life and wise stewardship, we nurture contemplative presence in the service of Church and society.*

If we were to reflect on the life of each of our members, the collective number of years served by the Benedictine Sisters of St. Paul's Monastery would probably number in the thousands. Moreover, we are fortunate to live a way of life shared by many men and women religious for over 1,500 years! Today, Benedictine values also continue to be lived by lay men and women who have dedicated their lives as Benedictine Associates and Oblates.

In the following pages you will find merely a glimpse of who we are and what we have accomplished with the grace of God over the past 25 years. You will hear varied voices — sisters and friends, associates and oblates — who reflect on their particular experience at St. Paul's Monastery. Every person we have encountered is part of our story; they know best how it has been a mutual blessing for us to encounter the Christ within them.

After 75 years, our daily commitment in all that we are and all that we do remains, "That in all things God may be glorified!" (I Peter 4:11).

Memoir of Many Voices

Lucia Schwickerath, OSB
General Editor

Seventy-five years ago, on June 22, 1948, 178 Benedictine women moved from St. Benedict's Convent in St. Joseph, Minnesota, to St. Paul to establish a new motherhouse which they named St. Paul's Priory. Like Benedict and his twin sister Scholastica of the fifth century, these young women responded to the Spirit. Their sense of adventure and their creative energy found a welcome home in our metropolitan diocese where the Catholic school system was booming, and Catholic healthcare centers were in their infant stages.

This book, focusing on the last 25 years of the Sisters of St. Paul's Monastery, is intended as a witness to the lived experiences of those sisters who dedicated themselves to God and lived their Benedictine values of prayer, hospitality, community, listening, moderation, and stability. Moreover, it poses the questions, "How have these inheritors of medieval monasticism adapted to the 21st century even as their numbers dwindled? What do they envision for the future to which God is calling them?" As the title suggests, these women will speak for themselves.

In the production of this book, God showed me that it is never too late to learn, be challenged, and take on new endeavors. As the stories came together, I was once again reminded of the many struggles and challenges our sisters faced. But as you read on, you will find that through prayer, hope, and a joyous spirit, we pulled together and continued to live the spirit of Benedict. With that as our guide, the last 25 years have been filled with growth and good works. Today, we not only honor the past, but look with prayerful hearts to a bright future.

God's hand can be seen and felt in the contributions made by so many. My team members on this project were the human hands guided by God as they helped record the journeys of individual sisters and the life and works of the community as a whole. This book is dedicated not only to family, friends, volunteers, and employees, but also to

God is inviting 21st century women to live Benedictine life in new ways.

those people who will bring fifth-century monasticism into the second half of this century, right up to our 100th anniversary.

We recognize that God is inviting women of this 21st century to live the Benedictine way of life in new ways. Our hope is to connect with readers whom God is calling, encouraging them as Benedict suggested, to "Listen with the ear of your heart!" The monastic *charism* (a gift from God which inspires others) can be lived in many ways — as a vowed religious, a Benedictine Associate, or an Oblate. Thus, with our eyes and hearts on the road before us, we have entitled the concluding section of this history, "Looking to the Future."

A final note. As Einstein reminded us, the boundaries of time, whether measured in years or minutes, can be nothing more than an illusion. Still, we find an anchor in being able to mark our growth, sometimes our loss, and with humility, our continuation. As you enter this story rooted in time, I invite you to be aware of its fluid boundaries. Some aspects of St. Paul's Monastery originated centuries ago and continue today; some began during this quarter of a century and continue, although in different form; others, while apparently ended, exist elsewhere. So, despite our best efforts at organization, time does not always divide neatly. A spiritual inspiration may appear on a sunny day, be realized during a challenging crisis, seem to diminish, or assume a different but blessed result. In other words, throughout this book you will hear repetition, echoes, and transformations.

Benedictine Sisters of St. Paul's Monastery

Chapter 1 – The Art of Listening

Marie Fujan, OSB Prioress 1996-2004

It has been good for me to take a closer look at my time as prioress of this Benedictine community, an eight-year period when our 25th anniversary commenced, the century turned, and the Priory became a Monastery. If I might begin with the summer of 1955 just before I entered St. Paul's Priory on Summit Avenue, you will perhaps better understand the title of my chapter.

That summer was flying by, and I spent my free time sewing new clothes for the start of college life at St. Benedict's College in St. Joseph, Minnesota. My friend, Jeanette, and I spent that last Labor Day at the neighboring town of Tracy, where at the Box-Car Day dance we met up with two male friends. The four of us had a great time until we learned that those two were going to the seminary in a couple of weeks — just our luck! But it did cause us to pause and ask them many questions! One of the boys suggested that we talk to Sister Terriselle, a Rochester Franciscan who had been very helpful in their discernment. After Sister Terriselle suggested that God might have used those great guys to help us change direction, we made an appointment with our pastor in Walnut Grove who, unknown to us, had been wondering all along whether we might have a religious vocation. Based on his recommendation, in a day or two we were on our way to visit the Franciscans in Rochester and the Benedictines in St. Paul.

That day the two convents were in stark contrast. The young Franciscan aspirants were already gone to study at the College of St. Teresa in Winona, Minnesota. Despite the graciousness of the sisters, their large motherhouse seemed lonely and cold without any young people. That afternoon, when we arrived at St. Paul's Priory, the Benedictine aspirants were playing volleyball outside in the driveway of the old mansion. In that welcome setting and after a warm conversation with Mother Marcelline Jung, Prioress, we happily received multiple papers for interested women: a form from a doctor, a list of weird clothes — white towels and black stockings — to bring, and a questionnaire regarding our future dreams and desires. Who says God does not have a sense of humor? As a result of listening to God, both Jeanette and I have been members of this Benedictine community for more than 60 years!

The prophets of old said it over and over: "Listen!" It was a favorite word of Jesus. My mother often sprinkled that word in when she really meant business. Moreover, St. Benedict opened his Rule with "Listen" and expected his followers to shape their lives by listening. Recently, I have been spending hours in our archives, inspired by information chronicled in *Passages*, our community newsletter, on the wonderful people and activities that danced through our lives during the years I was prioress. Thus, this chapter will capture the voices of others as well as some of my reminiscences from 1996 to 2004, offering me an opportunity to focus on the many ways we shared in God's plan. This reading, remembering, and research is indeed a unique way of listening.

I wish to begin my recollections of this community with the winter of 1997 when we changed our home's name from "Priory" — meaning "governed by a Prioress" — to "Monastery," thus claiming our centuries-old monastic heritage within the Catholic church. St. Benedict used the word "monastery" 72 times in his Rule. The name alteration clarified and confirmed our identity as monastics, persons who dedicate themselves to God, live in community under a Rule and a leader.

Two individuals who professed vows during my time as Prioress and continue to be blessings to our monastic community are Sister Jacqueline Leiter and Sister Linda Soler. It is always a joyous gift from God to welcome new members. Today Sister Jacqueline recounts her introduction to the Benedictine way of life: "Having grown up in Maplewood and attending Hill-Murray High School, I had been aware of St. Paul's Priory for most of my life, so often hearing the bell ringing for Midday Praise. I went off to college and then became busy beginning my teaching career, and the memory of the sound of the monastery bell calling sisters to prayer faded into the background. In the late nineties, the mother of one of my students who happened to be an oblate, invited me to visit the monastery. Out of curiosity, I accepted her invitation and later enrolled in the oblate program. I then saw that St. Paul's Monastery was a vibrant place where I could seek God while journeying with others. All my life I had been drawn to prayer and wanted to know God. I pronounced my first vows on the Feast of Saint Scholastica on February 10, 2004. I continue seeking God today, grateful to journey with my sisters and with oblates and associates." Still teaching, now English language learners and immigrant children, Sister Jacqueline also has some of her photography on display in the monastery art gallery.

Sister Jacqueline signs her vows on the altar as
Sister Marie, Prioress, witnesses.

Likewise, Sister Linda Soler, who completed her novitiate and pronounced final vows during my time of leadership, describes her final profession day: "As I stood before Prioress Sister Marie Fujan there was joy in my heart, knowing that my profession of these sacred vows was on the Feast of St. Benedict with my community, family, and friends as witnesses. After a couple of unsuccessful tries, Sister Marie placed the symbolic ring on my finger, and I received a community blessing. A particular memory I hold dear is that a white rose in memory of my mother was presented. The entire day was glorious, with a festive meal and a reception following."

Sister Linda Soler on profession day with her father,
George, and Sister Marie Fujan, Prioress.

An important part of our final profession ritual is that each member of the community greets and welcomes the newly professed sister. Hugs and smiles and immense joy abound! The day of our monastic profession is incredibly significant to each of us! On special anniversaries, such as Silver and Golden Jubilees, the whole monastic community celebrates together. Since God has blessed each of us with the gift of life, there is always a call for gratitude and celebration.

St. Benedict asks us to listen to the elders and provide exceptional care to the sick. It was important to me to have a private conversation with each sick sister regarding her particular needs. I recall a visit I made to one of our older sisters in the hospital. I asked if there was anything I could do for her. She said, "I would like the bed raised a little so we can talk together more easily." So, I walked around the bed two or three times trying to find something to push or pull to raise the head of the bed . . . and found nothing! We continued our visit and when I was about to leave, I made the mistake of saying, "Sister, is there anything I can do for you before I leave?" She replied, "No! You can't even raise my bed!"

Saying the final good-bye to a sister is often a mixture of grace and sorrow. It is especially hard when the deceased is a classmate and a good friend. So it was with Sister Veronica Novotny. *Passages* said of her, "She credited her Czech heritage for her love of song and dance and her readiness to find humor in life." While she was undergoing her third bout with cancer of the spine, she told me that she was going to offer her pain and suffering so that I would be a good prioress. What a touching gift. She was sixty years old when she went home to God. Such a beautiful person! A day or two after Sister Veronica died, I went across the hall to see Sister Leonardine. She was pretending to be asleep. I prayed, "Leonardine, I ask the Lord to bless you and I want you to know that I love you." She quickly opened her eyes and said, "I know that!" We both knew right where

What a touching gift!

we stood with each other. What a blessing! The Lord came for Sister Leonardine the next week.

Beginning in 1993, our downtown Benedictine Meditation Center offered a rich outreach program that rested upon the ancient Christian practice of centering prayer. It was in a building owned by Assumption Parish directly across from St. Joseph's Hospital in St. Paul. Eager to serve the urban world, Sister Mary White, a licensed psychotherapist, offered 20 minutes of centering prayer twice daily for government employees, business women and men, health care professionals, and visitors of all ages, races, nationalities, and faiths. In small groups people gathered at this haven to meditate after listening to a sacred reading or just a single word, followed by silence. "We don't speak; it's a time for us to be silent and let God speak to us," explains Sister Mary White.

Our Benedictine sisters and many dedicated volunteers provided helpful support for this contemplative practice, designing the meditation room, and assembling a small library for the many visitors who found the rare peace and quiet that we all need, especially in the heart of a big city, and the opportunity to come away refreshed and strengthened. During the decade of the Center's existence, many centering prayer groups were started in and around the metropolitan area. To extend the Center's outreach into the broader community, its staff and volunteers brought centering prayer to youth offenders at the Stillwater prison and into other detention and treatment centers. After the downtown Meditation Center's closing in 2003, many attendees continued as part of Minnesota Contemplative Outreach which even today brings seekers together. The benefits of the downtown Benedictine Meditation Center far exceeded the monastery's expectations.

Sister Mary White in the downtown Benedictine Meditation Center

Remember my friend Jeannette? Now a spiritual director, Sister Virginia Matter heard a desire from lay women wishing to live in community with the sisters, very much like some of our associates today. After conferring with me and the whole community, Sister Virginia and Sister Mary Lou Dummer received permission to begin an experimental interfaith community for lay women and sisters. In 1996, the community purchased a house for that purpose and named it "Peace Dwelling." As prioress, I, along with several other community members, blessed the home, prayed from room to room and then we closed the afternoon with socializing and laughing together. Two laywomen and two sisters lived at Peace Dwelling, and they opened their home to any community member for quiet and reflection.

Our sisters are also proud to have initiated the ministry of iLLUMINARE. This outreach ministry of spiritual renewal was directed toward lay ecclesial ministers, particularly parish liturgists, administrators, and directors of education in Minnesota and surrounding states. This decade-long program was made possible by a grant from the Lilly Foundation. Under the direction of Jacquelyne M. Witter, Ed. D., experienced ministers were provided advanced, ongoing formation that nourished and sustained their vocational call and commitment to excellence in ministry.

With our beautiful acres of open land, those ecclesial ministers and other retreatants enjoyed God's creation by walking on the earth. During my tenure, we designed our first labyrinth, a weaving pattern in the ground for walking meditation, dating as far back as 1000 AD. Jim Bartol and Sister Virginia Matter measured out the design and mowed the paths in the grass for several years. Today a second labyrinth of stone exists, thanks to friends of the monastery, designers Lise Moriarty and her husband who installed what is regarded as one of the most beautiful labyrinths in the Twin Cities. Everyone is invited to enjoy this opportunity for walking meditation as they listen to the birds singing in the quiet of creation.

Labyrinth at St. Paul's Monastery

Early in our history, the sisters listened to St. Benedict's wisdom regarding the importance of the arts and its preservation. Aware of how the arts enrich spirits and lighten hearts, St. Benedict devotes an entire chapter in his Rule to "Artisans of the Monastery." Indeed, cultivating beauty has always been part of the Benedictine monastic tradition as exemplified by the numerous hand-copied manuscripts and glowing illustrations by monk calligraphers as well as vibrant icons and paintings used to teach and adorn the ancient monastery walls where Benedict and his followers lived. Over the years, monastics practiced a variety of useful crafts and trades, making tools and other items such as elaborately embroidered altar cloths, sacred vessels, and hand-crafted vestments. St. Paul's Monastery continues this tradition: our sisters practice sewing, knitting, painting, sculpture, printmaking, pottery, singing, musical composition, card making, and photography.

Cultivating beauty has always been part of Benedictine monastic tradition!

From her travels throughout Europe in the 1950s, Sister Luanne Meagher brought back famous art pieces which then adorned our monastery walls. During my term of leadership, some of these magnificent works were originally displayed in a brightly lit lower-level hall of the Monastery. As I write, a beautiful gallery of art comprised of sculpture, oil paintings, etchings, charcoal, tapestry, pottery, and photography by our sisters and other living artists graces the front lobby area of our new monastery, a gift of the monastic community for retreatants and all God's people to enjoy. *Visio Divina* ("divine seeing") allows one, in particular our visitors at the Benedictine Center, to see with fresh vision, using sacred arts to open the "eye" of the heart. And the gallery artwork, with its changing exhibits, invites us to open our eyes to the wonder of the world and challenge injustices. The artist reminds us that "in all things, God may be glorified."

Monastery Art Gallery

In 2002 Jack Misenti and his wife Patty offered the community a 1 to 90 ratio, intricate, wooden model ship he built, depicting the one that brought Sisters Benedicta Riepp, Walburga Dietrick, and Maura Flieger to America in July 1852. The three sisters traveled from St. Walburg Abbey in Eichstatt, Bavaria, to this country to establish their first Benedictine motherhouse for Benedictine women in St. Marys, Pennsylvania. This model ship, too, is a form of art.

At the 2002 Easter Vigil, the sisters initiated the use of a new holy water font. Artist Sister Sarah Voss designed the wooden pedestal on which the bowl of blessed water rests. The bowl, made of fire clay stoneware with iron, was sculpted by community potter Sister Virginia Matter. Both the work of art and the artists continue to give glory to God — Sister Sarah in the heavenly kingdom and Sister

Visio Divina allows one to see with the "eye" of the heart.

Virginia in this kingdom on earth. In 2009, we gifted this font to the chapel at St. Therese Senior Community of Oxbow Lake in Brooklyn Park, Minnesota, where it still reminds residents of their own baptism.

Finally, and long before I became prioress, a 1911 Steinway grand piano stood in the monastery lobby as a decorative piece of furniture. In need of great repair, it was a gift to the sisters many years prior. Through the prayers of the sisters, the efforts of liturgist Sister Lucia Schwickerath, and the help of numerous and generous music lovers, the gorgeous Steinway was completely refurbished by Schmitt Music Company. We continue to be delighted by its full, rich tone and majestic appearance. Because the fundraising for this musical project was so successful, we were also able to purchase a model 795 Rodgers Organ to replace our old organ. As prioress, it was my honor to bless these instruments and then simply enjoy listening to beautiful music during the appreciation concert on Sunday, November 5, 2000!

Newly refurbished Steinway grand piano and new organ

I began my story with the word "Listen!" just as St. Benedict began his Holy Rule with that single word. All through my eight years as prioress, this was what I tried to do — listen. First, I listened to God, then to my sisters in community, and to my inner self. In turn, I sensed what God was asking of me and I chose to obey God daily, even when it meant being away from my duties for a month to take care of my health. During that time, I was blessed to have a team that stepped up to their tasks. I continue to be grateful! I am happy to say that God hears me today as I pray, pleading over and over, "Listen."

1996-2004 Leadership Team: Sisters Joan Utecht, Bernadine Frischmon, Sharon Schiller, Mary Lou Dummer, Marie Fujan. The lit candle signifies that we are counting on the help of the Lord at every meeting. The coffee cups speak of hospitality.

Chapter 2 – Crossing the Threshold

Carol Rennie, OSB Prioress 2004-2009

Sister Carol originally entered St. Benedict's Convent in St. Joseph, Minnesota, in 1956. She later joined St. Paul's Monastery in 1981. Today she has invited her colleague, Oblate Jeff Dols, to convey her story.

Early on, a tireless commitment to improving the effectiveness of religious education teachers took Sister Carol Rennie all over the world. Her path of teaching teachers virtually crisscrossed the globe. It was after receiving a Master of Arts degree in Religious Education from the University of Notre Dame that she began leading religious education workshops, the first being in Puerto Rico. Within a few months she was called to Alaska to work with Sunday school teachers on Army and Air Force bases in Anchorage and Fairbanks. This initial military involvement led to more workshops in Germany and Italy and projects with the Navy that took Sister Carol to Okinawa, Hawaii, and Spain. "Overseas military bases sensed a need to provide meaningful church experiences for people whose lives were encountering the transiency of relocation and the strains of foreign living," she explained.

The framework of much of her work is the National Teacher Education Program (NTEP), founded by Dr. Locke E. Bowman Jr., a program Sister Carol was affiliated with for 11 years, 1974-1985. The association took her to Louisville Presbyterian Theological Seminary in Kentucky, where she was director of the Teacher Education Laboratory from 1974-1977. The experience there was so significant that Sister Carol said, "It was like living a lifetime in three years." Living in a Presbyterian community was a new experience, but "definitely one that confirmed my Catholic faith," she recalled.

Sister Carol has worked with religious denominations almost as varied as the places where she has taught. She recalled an instance of a project with the Armenian Church in New York: "We had a task force of 30 people who listened to priests explain major conceptual beliefs and then converted the information to lesson plans." This was a productive, creative time. She wrote courses of study including more than two hundred individualized instruction units about liturgy and more than eighteen packets on concepts such as faith, hope, peace, forgiveness, covenant, and discipleship. All the instructional materials she developed were piloted in the laboratories she directed. They then were published by NTEP and were available throughout the country ("Sister Carol Rennie Thrives on Teaching the Art of Teaching," 4).

Whether in the role of academician or administrator, Sister Carol's style was one of a true teacher, acting most often as a catalyst. She maintained that the essence of effective teaching skills does not change with time. "Instead, I hope that we are always improving and doing what we know better," she said. Sister Carol's roles at St. Paul's Monastery tended to draw upon her natural gifts of teacher and wise

"It was like living a lifetime in three years."

counselor. As Oblate Director, she was instrumental in embellishing the oblate program to include more structure and content in both the initial and ongoing oblate formation and education. She was also key in the movement to add lay leadership to the oblates.

Sister Carol served as Director of the Benedictine Center from 2000-2004, identifying its ministry "as a sacred threshold between St. Paul's Monastery and the wider world." She said, "As I live in this space, I am called to savor the 'in-betweenness' of life and ministry." She dearly valued the inclusion of the laity in teaching and ministry. Recognizing and affirming the gifts of those who served, she placed a high priority on inviting professional and spiritually deep persons onto the monastery's staff. Not only did she heed Benedict's call to hospitality as she radiated welcoming each visitor as Christ, but she also affirmed each individual and all staff personnel to be the best they could.

As a spiritual director, Sister Carol continued her role as a stimulus to those whom she led, both meeting with individuals and small groups as well as conducting peer supervision of spiritual directors. She initiated an evening of Taizé Prayer, simple chants based on the scriptures followed by periods of silence — a time to create an environment for encountering the Mystery of God. She took part in a program called "Great Conversations," for she saw conversation as having the power to inspire and transform, as one explores how God may be moving in one's life. The Holy Rule was her foundation, and she wrote reflections on the Rule of Benedict in her notebook with drawings and calligraphy. "Throughout her ministry she had special words which were very meaningful to her," said Sister Virginia Matter. "Cherishing the path of *Uncertainty*, she loved the meaning of *Threshold Moments*. She brought these into her spiritual direction and teaching. Each year she designed a retreat called *Crossing the Threshold* for persons leaving the old year and moving into the new year. Later she changed the name to *On the Crest.*"

As prioress, Sister Carol's term coincided with one of the most important processes in the history of St. Paul's Monastery: the building of a new, smaller monastery at 2675 Benet Road and the sale of the Larpenteur Avenue monastery and surrounding land. Sister Carol led and monitored the progress of multiple planning and implementation committees and task forces, comprised of both sisters and lay participants. And all this activity was in addition to the regular day-to-day duties of serving as prioress.

Sketch of proposed new monastery

During the years 2004-2009, the monastic community of St. Paul's Monastery was deeply engaged in strategic planning and discernment over questions about the community's future and its property. A financial and demographic study was commissioned, and the results that became evident were clearly stated: membership was declining as was the number of sisters earning salaries; operation and maintenance costs would continue to increase; income would decrease. As the planning committees met, they determined the need for further study of their facilities, buildings, and land. Throughout the summer and fall of 2004, the sisters met in dialogue sessions with Tubman Family Alliance and CommonBond Communities. As the groups met, they kept in mind the values they held sacred: hospitality, prayer, community, a balanced life, contemplative spirit, and their identity as Benedictine monastic women of St. Paul's Monastery.

By 2005, the sisters had made important decisions: they approved the sale of their 59% share of the building and land to Hill-Murray School; they invited Tubman and CommonBond to visit the monastery and campus to continue conversation regarding their plans for use of the building and land; and they determined they should build a new monastery sized to their future needs. At the February 2006 chapter meeting, the sisters approved the sale of land to CommonBond and authorized the Implementation Committee and Monastery Board of Directors to proceed with negotiations to sell the monastery on Larpenteur Avenue to Tubman Family Alliance. By 2008 Sister Carol oversaw a flurry of activity related to the new monastery: necessary permits from the city of Maplewood, approval of the plans of the Pope Design Group, groundbreaking and construction by McGough, final sale of the building to Tubman, and the opening of two new streets — Monastery Way and Benet Road.

Finally, on February 10, 2009, the Feast of Scholastica, the sisters moved across campus to their new monastery. After fourteen years of discernment and ten months of construction, they created a beautiful, simple building they now called "home." In establishing their new monastery, the sisters committed to "move into the future with hope to co-create the vision to which God is calling them."

Groundbreaking Ceremony for the New Monastery

Amid this milestone event in the life of the monastic community stood Sister Carol and her steady leadership as prioress. "She knew how to collaborate and call persons into their gifts, and delegated well, respecting their ability to carry it out," said Sister Virginia. "Her staff for the new building consisted of the most professional, competent people one could hope for." Her steady sense of confidence is captured in this statement from the close of her 2007 annual report: "The sisters have confidence in God as they believe and live the words of the Prophet Jeremiah, which have been the mantra throughout the many years of their strategic planning: 'I know the plans I have for you, says our God, plans for your good, plans to give you a future full of hope'" (Jeremiah 29:11).

Sister Carol found the meaning of her time as prioress expressed in this language in response to the Book of Ruth, "Wherever You Go, I Shall Go." "When the time of our particular sunset comes, our things, our accomplishments won't really matter a great deal. However, the clarity and care with which we have loved and served others will speak with vitality of the great gift of life we have been privileged to receive and offer to others" ("Wherever You Go" 1972).

Sister Leanne Meartz and Sister Carol Rennie celebrate Holy Thursday Liturgy

Chapter 3 – A Beacon of Hope

Lucia Schwickerath, OSB Prioress 2009-2014

My story begins, or I should say "continues," on June 15, 2009. As the sisters were becoming accustomed to their new home, I was in a state of disbelief and dismay. For the first time, I was sitting in the high-backed chair in the Prioress' office, while the same thought repeated itself over and over: "I'm Marie Schwickerath . . . I don't know how to be prioress!" I found myself mesmerized by the glass mobile hanging above me, each of its fifty-two crystals representing a sister and each sparkling in the morning sun. My amazement was tempered by uncertainty, for the future was truly unknown. But suddenly I thought, "I have no time to daydream! I need to get on with my work before Morning Praise!"

Soon I would celebrate 50 years as a Benedictine sister. It all seemed surreal, including the day I had left on the train from our little farming town of New Hampton, Iowa, to begin a new adventure. I would be a stenographer for the FBI in Washington, D.C., a job I had dreamed of since fifth grade. I loved my work and the new friends I made while living in our nation's capital. Even though I had planned to marry and raise a family, God had other plans for me that would bring me back to the Midwest, this time to Minnesota. After much prayer and discernment, I said "yes" to God. On September 8, 1957, my family brought me to the front door of St. Paul's Priory at 301 Summit Avenue in St. Paul. That day I joined the Benedictine community. And now, beginning yet another of life's adventures as prioress, that same question I had asked myself when I lived in

Washington, D.C., and again when I joined St. Paul's Monastery, is tugging at my heart: "Why did God bring me to this place?"

In 1965, we left that Priory on Summit Avenue and moved to our second home on Larpenteur Avenue in Maplewood, living there until the 2009 completion of this current monastery nearby on Benet Road. The sisters were excited and enjoying the new environment with its light woodwork and polished floors although many still longed for their past home. This contemporary monastery was three stories of golden Mankato stone culminating in a bell tower and extending to a circular chapel, with a single-story wing of retreat bedrooms to one side. It seems as though at every turn its windows open to peaceful and comforting light. At the front door one enters a world of sacred art: an illuminated manuscript of the Benedictine Rule rests just inside for all to read, within a surrounding gallery of sacred art that ushers the guest or the sister right to the holy water font in front of the open chapel. Our oval chapel is designed with many subtle and enveloping curves which reflect the spirituality of Christian women. Its two facing sides enhance the voices of the sisters as they sing the psalms in antiphonal style. Thin, rectangular and larger square windows near the ceiling offer glimpses of the gently rolling grounds with statues, maple and oak trees, gardens, and a labyrinth made of Mankato stone matching the monastery's stone construction. In fact, when you stand at the lectern to read the scriptures, you can view the huge wrought-iron cross that stands in the sisters' cemetery.

I planned to marry and raise a family; God had other plans!

Our focus on the beauty and preservation of nature in all of God's creation led the way for new ecological endeavors, including the green roof, reflective glass windows, and water-saving devices throughout the community grounds. The Sacred Ground Initiative has provided a prayerful outdoor environment for sisters and guests alike. A winding path encircles parallel rows of the simple headstones of all our deceased sisters. Nearby, the infirm sisters who are lovingly cared for in the monastery Healthcare Center can view this area where some day they will be buried alongside their companions. That same path gracefully leads to the Fatima Grotto, relocated from the former St. Joseph Orphanage on Randolph Avenue where in earlier years our sisters nurtured orphaned children. The statue of St. Benedict, however, holds a prominent place, standing tall in the center of a memorial plaza. Berms create an undulating landscape, providing a spacious playground for wildlife while protecting retreatants from noise and visual distraction. Statues of Francis, Mary, and Joseph also overlook these sacred grounds.

St. Benedict created by artist Linda Dabeau,
donated by Jack and Cathy Farrell

St. Francis

Fatima Grotto

Blessed Virgin Mary sculptured
by Sister Irene Uptegrove

St. Joseph with Jesus

Surrounded by all this beauty, I certainly had no time for nostalgia! God had called me to this place for some reason and, as the new prioress I knew I had to follow the wise words of Sister Luanne, one of our many instructors. She often called us to class with, "This is no time to dilly-dally!" My first task was to appoint the leadership team, a custom at the time. I immediately realized how invaluable their advice would be. Sister Linda Soler, Subprioress, contributed an extra spark of energy and playful spirit to all of us. With Sister Mary Courteau as treasurer, I had no need to worry: her experience in the field of finance was extensive. Sister Mary White, a professional counselor, gave me personal support just as she did to each sister in times of concern or worry.

2004-2009 Leadership Team with crystal mobile. Sisters Mary Courteau, Mary White, Linda Soler, and Lucia Schwickerath.

With our move to Benet Road, a newly configured campus had formed. Tubman Family Alliance became the new owner and occupier of our former monastery and CommonBond Communities purchased and developed property we had once owned. In effect, our spiritual impact was broadened; it was as though "A Beacon of Hope" had been quietly created in the east metro.

At once our charism of hospitality burst forth as the first open house invitation went out to staff and residents of Tubman, a shelter which provides services for families and individuals fleeing domestic violence. We also invited residents from the CommonBond affordable housing for families and seniors.

Aerial view of the Beacon of Hope campus

Next, greeting them not so much as new neighbors but simply in a new setting, we welcomed two groups that had been housed on our property for years: Hill-Murray School, originally known as Archbishop Murray Memorial High School, and Maple Tree Childcare Center. The Hill-Murray teachers, support staff, and students enjoyed a typical Benedictine open house with prayer, tours, refreshments, and conversation. The children and caregivers from the daycare center next door partied with the sisters, enjoying treats in the big dining room. The high-pitched voices of children rang joyfully throughout the whole monastery as they do to this very day when the little ones come to visit the sisters. We, along with these organizations, are truly a "Beacon of Hope" which shines brightly today as we celebrate our 75th anniversary. All the neighbors on Monastery Way continue as a community dedicated to our mission to serve women, children, seniors, and those in need.

Hill-Murray School

Maple Tree Childcare Center

Tubman Family Alliance

CommonBond Communities

St. Paul's Monastery: a place of prayer and work

Celebrations were aplenty that first year, with each festivity taking on a unique character. There were open houses for members of our families of origin, for friends, and for employees. We welcomed Benedictine sisters and brothers from the monasteries of St. Benedict's in St. Joseph, Minnesota, St. Bede in Eau Claire, Wisconsin, and St. John's Abbey of Collegeville, Minnesota. They are our religious family! Our charter members had come from their home at St. Benedict's Convent in 1948 to open the first Benedictine Priory in St. Paul, thereby making St. Benedict's our "Grandmother House," as I call it. Likewise, the community of St. Bede was founded on June 21, 1948, the day before our founding, making them our "Country Cousins," as I lovingly call them. They, in turn, sometimes call us their "City Cousins!"

Next, our former members came for a reunion. They came not only to see us and our new home, but to share the many ways they had been enriched while living with us. Some spoke of the lifelong practices they formed while in community, leading them to continue to actively live and spread the Good News of Christ and our Benedictine Charism. We spoke at length about the concept of a "temporary call to community," and about their multiple calls in one lifetime. We had grieved and felt a loss whenever one of our members left, not realizing that it was part of God's great plan.

"All guests who present themselves are to be welcomed as Christ" *(RB 53:1).*

St. Benedict reminds us that "All guests who present themselves are to be welcomed as Christ" (RB 53:1). Very early on, the sisters realized that people from the greater community were essential in facilitating the mission of our sisters. One of the first groups formed and welcomed by those 1948 charter members was a Lay Advisory Board. I am happy to say that active lay involvement continued during my tenure as prioress and is still an essential part of monastery life. Our Justice and Peace Committee, which continues to this day, intentionally partners with those who serve women, children, and others in need. Oblates and other lay friends serving on this committee extend a Benedictine welcome to all by their involvement in the Twin Cities community and beyond. As a testament to our shared values, a Peace Pole with the inscription "May Peace Prevail on Earth" in twelve languages was secured by this committee, blessed, and planted on our property in the summer of 2009. "*PAX*," peace, is a 1500-year-old Benedictine motto.

Peace Pole

When 2010 arrived, the sisters were happy to celebrate our traditional New Year's Day Community Party, an annual gathering day for our own family of sisters. With all the newness, transitions, and events of the previous year, this community celebration enabled us to bond even more closely. We reminisced about Christmas at the former monasteries and enjoyed sharing more recent stories. We had a wonderful time! "Thank you, God, for bringing me to this place!"

However, the happiness lingering from our New Year's celebration soon vanished. Newspaper headlines flashed: "U.S. Nuns Facing Vatican Scrutiny" and "Cardinal Franc Rode announces an Apostolic Visitation for U.S. Catholic Sisters." In response to this 2009-2013 Vatican-imposed Visitation, Catholic laity generated a hurricane of support: "Don't monkey with our Sisters!" and "Nuns Rock!" were typical headlines. Certain bishops and cardinals were concerned that Catholic sisters might

Sister Louise Inhofer and her sister, Sister Mary Claire enjoy celebrating together

be straying from legitimate church teaching, stretching rules while living and teaching false Catholic doctrine. To investigate these so called "unlawful practices," all communities of Catholic religious women in the United States were required to complete a written Apostolic questionnaire. In addition, some religious communities were chosen at random for on-site visitation. This news spread throughout the world, creating a blanket of suspicion over religious women in the United States. Naturally, laity, especially those nurtured and educated by religious sisters, resented this unfair and inaccurate accusation. One survey identified more than 1700 individuals eager to give testimony regarding the significance that religious women had in their lives.

The Benedictine prioresses were accustomed to gathering annually to address current issues and share common challenges. I remember this group discerning at length and deciding with intention which sections of the questionnaire they would and would not complete. You see, the Apostolic Delegation for Religious addresses canonical issues, those relating to religious life, such as prayer, vows, and community charism.

Finances, land, and property are secular issues, not within the authority of an apostolic visitation. After prayer and further discernment, each Benedictine Community of sisters in our Federation was advised to complete the canonical section of the questionnaire but intentionally omit the secular sections.

The final 2014 Apostolic Visitation official report reads in part, "Convinced of the sublime dignity and beauty of the consecrated life, may we all pray for and support our women religious and actively promote vocations to the religious life" ("Conclusion" September 8, 2014). Later in November that same year, Pope Francis declared the "Year of Consecrated Life." In an "Apostolic Letter to all Consecrated people" his inspiring words were directed to young and old, lay as well as monastic, indeed "the whole Christian people," energetically calling us to renew gratitude and commitment. "Live the present with passion" he urged, and "especially in the West sustain hope in the face of current uncertainties." He praised the old saying, "Where there are religious, there is joy" and continued, "I am counting on you to 'wake up the world' since the distinctive sign of consecrated life is prophesy. I told the Superiors General: 'Radical evangelical living is not only for religious: it is demanded of everyone. But religious follow the Lord in a special way, in a prophetic way'" (Pope Francis "Expectations for the Year of Consecrated Life" II 2).

Pope Francis' words have seemed to me a beacon of hope which always shone brightly during my five years as Prioress, even during times of challenge. Thus, the song *"Wake the World with Dawning Joy,"* inspired by this 2014 papal letter, continues to move me.

When Tubman grew and began to use office spaces we had been allowed to continue to occupy, we found a way to reconfigure our workplace in the new monastery. Due to financial constraints, we saw the dissolution or transition of a few ministries, many of which now exist in a new form or under new leadership. This period of adjustments and trials was actually a time of opportunity for innovation, growth, and spiritual enlightenment. The wonderful Associate program welcoming lay women to companion more closely with vowed religious became a reality in 2014 and the relationships continue to grow stronger each year. Our Oblate ministry obviously flourished under the direction of shared lay leadership whose contributions have been invaluable to the program and its participants. The Benedictine Center, established before my tenure, thrived by engaging in significant partnerships and adding innovative programs that attracted many guests to the monastery. So, while these were challenging times, they were also times of immense blessings, growth, and joy. As the title of this chapter suggests, during these five years the sisters, the new monastery, and the whole campus began to shine as an ever-present beacon of hope.

During my lifetime, this young woman from Iowa who had envisioned a vastly different life for herself, found the life she was meant to live by saying "yes" to God early on and following His plan daily. Thankfully, my story continues. Now, instead of asking, "Why did God bring me to this place?" I can honestly say I understand more than ever that "I am exactly where I'm supposed to be."

Wake the World with Dawning Joy

based on the words of Pope Francis to the Consecrated Religious of the world.
Commissioned by the National Religious Vocation Conference and VISION Vocation Guide
in honor of the Year of Consecrated Life.

BERGOGLIO
7.6.7.6.8.8.8.7.

Steven C. Warner

Strident ♩ = 96

1. Wake the world with dawn-ing joy! Wake it with your glad-ness!
2. Though the world is locked in sleep, Let us rise re - joic-ing!
3. Love the world with dif - frent eyes, God's own love in - car-nate!
4. Thun - der now God's song of praise, wake to harp and danc-ing,

Work for jus - tice, live in peace, Claim the Word cour - a - geous! Let us
One with Christ, his light to keep, Called to hu - man kind - ness. Let us
Leav - ing all to fol - low Christ: Sweet and end - less mer - cy! Let us
Song to lift us all our days, Song of love and tri - umph! For the

sing to God this new day, see the world in a dif - frent way. Let us wake the world,
sing to God this new day, walk the world in a ho - ly way, Let us wake the world,
sing to God this new day, reach the world in mir-a-cu-lous ways, Let us wake the world,
Bride - groom now a - waits us, in the fa - ces of all we meet, Now a - wake the world!

wake the world, with a - bid - ing words of faith.
wake the world, with up - lift - ing words of hope.
wake the world, with pro - phe - tic words of love.
Wake the world, with un - end - ing words of joy.

Chapter 4 – "If today you hear God's voice, harden not your heart" (Psalm 95).

Paula Hagen, OSB Prioress 2014-2019

This admonition from St. Benedict's Prologue to the Rule — "If today you hear God's voice, harden not your heart" — has influenced my faith and my entire life as a vowed Benedictine religious. On June 8, 2014, I was installed as prioress of our community and for the next five years it was my privilege and sacred responsibility to lead our 35 sisters. From approving feast day schedules to strategic planning for our future, the needs of our community were my constant companions and concerns.

Installation of Sister Paula as prioress with Federation President
Susan Hutchens and former prioress, Sister Lucia

I was a Bird Island, Minnesota, farm girl, the oldest girl in a family of seven children. I learned leadership skills right alongside my older brother and best friend James, partly out of necessity as we worked together on the farm, gathering wood for the stove in our little red wagon, and because taking charge seemed to fit our personalities. We were also very supportive of our younger siblings whom we loved playing with. It is not surprising that the profession I later chose involved empowering the next generation. I learned from my family of nine both the value of teamwork and the value of community.

Sister Paula and her brother James

I have been asked often why I chose to become a vowed religious, and my answer is simple: I felt God's invitation and responded. I have found that God reveals God's loving presence to each person in unique ways. I saw the value of a Christ-centered life, for Christ had been a very real presence in our family. Later, on September 8, 1956, in obedience to this call and with great anticipation, I joined the Sisters of St. Benedict of St. Paul's Priory. I had already completed my first year at the College of St. Catherine and earned a full scholarship for the remaining baccalaureate years. After the novitiate, our prioress, Sister Marcelline Jung, discerned that I should return to complete my major in Occupational Therapy; at that time of the rampant polio epidemic, she foresaw this new profession becoming a crucial part of health care. My training certainly broadened my perspective on health care: the challenge with each patient was to see the potential in that person's body and spirit, regardless of age or disabilities. This generous scholarship opened many professional doors and ministry opportunities for me and as my professional challenges changed, I kept discovering greater, new potential in each situation and individual. This discovery, as well as my own personal relationship with God, were the great joys in my life.

During my first ten years as a registered occupational therapist, I was assigned to minister in our hospital and nursing home in Winsted, Minnesota, and then at St. Joseph's Home for Children in Minneapolis. After serving as a family minister in St. Joseph's parish in New Hope, Minnesota, I was struck by how much additional support families with a child with a disability needed than my occupational therapy skills could provide. As a result, I was able to pursue a Master's degree in Occupational Therapy and Family Systems at Colorado State University in Fort Collins. Together, these studies allowed me to comprehend the deep need each child has for supportive adults who not only provide unique skills for daily living, but also help the child develop as a total person.

In 1983, the prioress, Sister Duane Moes, was invited by our Sister Rosemary Rader to visit and witness the needs of families in St. Timothy's Catholic Parish in Mesa, Arizona. I was then assigned to St. Timothy's where I came to recognize the crucial need of our young families for guidance and encouragement. Consequently, I developed the curriculum and materials for Ministry of Mothers Sharing (MOMS) in 1986. The concepts of this vital ministry shaped by Benedictine values were based on my conviction that motherhood is a call to holiness. Designed to serve the varying needs of many mothers (as many as 500,000), it also motivated them to be leaders and continue their own spiritual growth. As a result, wisdom of their vocation as mothers deepened. My affiliation with Christine Jurisich led to our collaborative leading of retreats in English and Spanish for mothers and grandmothers. Thus, a national office of MOMS was established at the monastery until 2013 where I served as a retreat leader until I became prioress the following year. Today the contemporary version of this ministry of retreats and workshops for all women continues nationally in the form of *Retreat, Reflect, Renew* under the leadership of Christine Jurisich.

"My experience with Ministry of Mothers Sharing invited me to a different way of life as a Catholic, a wife, and mother," says Christine Jurisich.

Let us return to June 8, 2014, Pentecost Sunday, the day I succeeded Sister Lucia Schwickerath as prioress. Just a few days later, on June 20, our Subprioress, Sister Mary Lou Dummer, and I celebrated our 60th Jubilee as Sisters of St. Benedict! Because of my deep commitment to Benedictine spirituality, I moved with great enthusiasm into this new position.

The main accomplishments and joys from my term as prioress were four-fold: the development of a five-year strategic plan to direct our community's goals, ministries, and finances; the Federation Visitation at our monastery; a new annual celebration on the Feast of St. Scholastica honoring a lay volunteer who is supportive of our Benedictine life; and the many festivities throughout the year in observation of our community's 70th anniversary. A professional strategic-planning consultant collaborated with the Monastic Council, monastery department heads, and volunteers to create our five-year plan which was then implemented by a strategic committee. For us, strategic planning is truly a call to discern what we envision as God's plan for us over the next five years — not a simple or facile task. Just a few of the important outcomes of our 2014 -2019 strategic plan included a 5-to-10-year financial projection, development of interpersonal communication best practices, a focus on membership, and the formation of a committee to evaluate future uses of our monastic space and facilities.

With the anchor of our strategic plan in place, the Federation Visitation, which is a spiritual "audit" of the religious life and health of the vowed community, followed. We invited a team of sisters from other Benedictine monasteries to offer their support to our community in the form of affirmations of continuing good practices as well as their recommendations for improvement. As prioress, I found great value in the advice of these experienced sisters. They offered our community untold encouragement and insight.

On February 10, 2018, the community celebrated the Feast of St. Scholastica, the twin sister of Benedict. On that day we awarded our wonderful friend and volunteer Julianna Sandin the first St. Scholastica Award for her extraordinary contributions to our community. Julianna, her family, and friends joined us for Eucharist and a festive meal. Since 2008, Julianna has blessed us in many ways, especially by her fidelity to the sisters living in our Healthcare Center.

On June 22, 2018, we began the celebration of the 70th year of our founding. By planning, serving, and praying, sisters were integrally involved in all aspects of each celebration throughout 2018. The first festivity opened with the celebration of the Eucharist in the Hill-Murray School Chapel with Archbishop Bernard Hebda presiding. After campus tours, including a display of our pre-Vatican II habit, we and our guests enjoyed Bridgeman's ice cream on our patio, courtesy of a generous donor.

Sisters Susan, Eleanor, Louise, Margaret, Lois, LaVerne, Archbishop Hebda; Sisters Lucia, Marie, Paula, Mary Lou, Virginia, Linda; Jacqueline, Carol, Catherine Nehotte, Mary, Joan

This community was enthusiastic, involved, and ready for more 70th anniversary celebrations! Hospitality is our Benedictine charism, and we choose to express our gratitude to God by festive celebrations — celebrating with those whose joy we share as well as with those who are eager to share ours. So, July 7 saw another reunion, this time at our original Priory home at 301 Summit Avenue where we had gardened, cooked, washed, prayed, chanted, and lived in monastic community for 17 years. The Germanic American Institute, current owner, welcomed us and all the guests we had invited from our founding community of St. Benedict's with German cakes and beverages. Naturally, we roamed the grounds on Summit Avenue, reminiscing about the different rooms in the mansions, including, of course, the red stairs.

Sisters Paula and Mary Lou with guests from St. Benedict's
Monastery at our first priory on Summit Avenue.

August of 2018 allowed us to welcome back former sisters of St. Paul's Monastery. Each invited guest shared photos and a personal update while enjoying *hors d'oeuvres*. Much reminiscing continued during the delicious meal. The evening closed with Evening Praise and many promises to stay in touch. It was a blessed day of reconnection, surely a response to Benedict's words and the plea of the psalmist: "If today you hear God's voice, harden not your heart."

We ended our year of community anniversary festivities in September when we invited the Archdiocesan and St. John's clergy to an "Octoberfest for Clergy." These priests who had so faithfully met our spiritual needs day after day and Sunday after Sunday by presiding at Eucharist enjoyed a traditional fall dinner followed by Evening Praise. In particular, Abbot John Klassen from St. John's and Father Bob Schwartz, one of our daily chaplains, regaled us with stories of those early days. Sister Marie Fujan composed and performed a song for the occasion, sharing our hopes for an uplifting future. These reunions not only demonstrate Benedictine hospitality, but also offer us a special opportunity to praise and thank God for our long-lived relationships.

Finally, in 2019, to my surprise, we were invited to apply for and subsequently received an "Advancing Mission 2.0: Women Religious in the 21st Century" grant in support of Catholic sisters building a culture of mission advancement and outreach to new donors and benefactors. Gerald and Henrietta Rauenhorst and the Hilton Foundation provided three years of funding for intense leadership training as well as professional and financial services to advance Benedictine best fundraising practices. We joined representatives from ten other communities for training and for in-person, annual meetings at the School of Philanthropy in Indianapolis. There we received support from other grant recipients and from grant administrators themselves. Fortunately, after a year-long audit of our mission advancement strengths, challenges, opportunities, and needs, we were able to hire a Communications Coordinator responsible for updating our technological 21st century communication. That audit empowered us to reach out to the larger community and share the Benedictine values of work and prayer. For me, this professional training and support was a dream come true, just what we needed, motivating us to work together to promote the Benedictine charism to a broader audience, the world.

On May 5, 2019, this Benedictine community, in the presence of the Federation President, installed Sister Catherine Nehotte as the 12th prioress of St. Paul's Monastery. The very next day at Morning Praise, she, along with all the sisters, blessed me as I left for a six-month sabbatical. The joys and challenges of having led our community will always remain for me a sacred memory and a special gift from God and the sisters.

Chapter 5 – An Unprecedented Time

Catherine Nehotte, OSB Prioress 2019 -2024

E ach of my predecessors has shared her story as prioress. Being in the midst of my service in this role, I cannot tell you how it will end. What I can tell you is how it all began.

I started my education at Visitation School in South Minneapolis, which was staffed by the Sisters of St. Benedict of St. Paul's Priory. It was Sister Francis Oeffling, my first-grade teacher, who inspired my vocation. One would not expect a child of six to be impacted by a teacher who would help to set the course of her life, but that was the case for me. I could see God's love and peace emanating from her. Sister Francis welcomed us as Christ would have. I came to find out that this was a charism of the Sisters of St. Benedict.

A significant change occurred when I transferred to public schools for grades five through twelve when I realized that not everyone was Catholic. I then attended the University of St. Thomas in St. Paul, Minnesota, earning a bachelor's degree in Business. Father Robert Wellisch, my English teacher, was a contact for a January interim course offered at the priory entitled *"Ora et Labora."* I had not known that he was also the weekday chaplain at St. Paul's Priory, nor that Sister Lucia Schwickerath was the coordinator of the interim. Sister Lucia had been a music teacher whom I remembered from Visitation School. That month of my living at the priory, now known as St. Paul's Monastery, provided an experience of the Benedictine life of work and prayer. God blessed me by reconnecting me with the order of sisters who had taught me so many years ago.

The following January, I explored the Franciscan order by serving the people of Vanceburg, Kentucky. I came to realize that my calling was to join the Benedictine Sisters of St. Paul's Priory. I worked until I was able to pay off my student loans and have sufficient funds to get me through the formation years as a postulant and novice. I then professed first vows and was called to work in the finance office. Later, I was blessed with the opportunity to be educated as a nationally certified massage therapist. One of the gifts of community is that you are invited to do things that you would never imagine doing. Under the leadership of Sister Carol Rennie, I served as the Oblate Director for initial formation. It is so life-giving to know that God is calling lay men and women of all faiths to learn about and live the Benedictine charism. The Holy Spirit is definitely working in that we are blessed with new oblates each year. Also, the Associate ministry continues to grow in number. It is an opportunity for single, Catholic women to live Benedictine values in closer association with our community while living in their own homes.

Prior to my election, I had served as the community Treasurer and worked in Human Resources at both the Minneapolis and Maplewood locations of Tubman where they provide comprehensive services to families and individuals fleeing domestic violence and in need of shelter services. It supports clients through their long-term healing processes and helps them overcome barriers through its core service areas: shelter and housing, mental and chemical health, legal services, youth programs, and work-shops and support groups. Tubman has now consolidated all its residential services into our former monastery building.

Sister Catherine on her installation day with former prioresses:
Sisters Rosemary, Marie, Duane, Lucia, Eleanor, Catherine, Carol, Paula

The sisters of St. Paul's Monastery have always believed that God helps us choose the prioress who is needed for the time. In 2019, when I was elected prioress, I was shocked! How could this happen? I recalled the words of my mother, "Do the best you can. God asks no more of anyone." My father, who had died three months prior to my election, predicted, "They're going to ask even more of you."

Sister Catherine with her father, Robert

I knew that the only way I could do this new assignment, which was clearly taking me out of my comfort zone, was with the grace of God. Nonetheless, this role affords me many opportunities for growth. I was prioress for only ten months when the COVID-19 pandemic struck. The monastery needed to go on total lockdown. Closing the doors of our retreat center was a necessary but difficult decision since one of our most beloved Benedictine charisms is hospitality.

However, this time of enclosure blessed me, affording me the opportunity to preside at Word Communion Services when we were unable to have priests preside at Eucharist. Especially meaningful was presiding at the final rites of some of the sisters who died during my term, though fortunately, none of them died because of COVID-19. Technology such as Zoom and live streaming gave us the opportunity to share rituals, reflections, and remembrances of these sisters with their friends and relatives.

One particular challenge during my term of office has been to consider the financial solvency of our retreat center, the Benedictine Center. We know that our COVID-19 restriction policy has prevented some people from reserving space for meetings or retreats. Therefore, the retreat ministry is presently supported by the monastery in that we are not currently requiring a facility fee.

Another successful ministry of the monastery is the Maple Tree Childcare Center which is housed in our former laundry building. The Maple Tree Childcare Center has faithfully served families for more than 30 years and continues to provide a safe, peaceful environment for infants, toddlers, and preschoolers. You may be one of those children or know someone who played under the famous maple tree at 2625 Benet Road, Maplewood, Minnesota.

Children from the Maple Tree Childcare Center help celebrate Sister Catherine's birthday

As I continue to serve in my role as prioress, I am learning daily that there is a hunger for spirituality in our world today. With the support of the grace of God and a balance of precautions, we continue to do well the work we love. There are times when I have had to do or say things that are not popular, but it is important to me to stay true to my convictions and protect the lives of our sisters. While I experience a full range of emotions in this role, God knows my heart and is guiding me in each step. I have learned to have a sense of humor about almost everything. It is God's way of helping me not take myself too seriously. Another great blessing!

There is a hunger for spirituality in our world today.

Chapter 6 – Living a Vowed Life:
A Choice to Say "Yes" to God

Vowed Sisters

Out of love, a vowed Benedictine sister dedicates herself totally to God in service of God's people as lived out through the three vows of Obedience, Stability, and Fidelity to the Monastic Way of Life. She is called by God to live out these vows in a specific religious community (Stability). She willingly changes her life in any way necessary to follow God (Fidelity to the Monastic Way of Life), and lives under the Rule of St. Benedict and a prioress (Obedience). A woman chooses this way of life after discovering a call from God which manifests itself uniquely to each person.

As we sat together one afternoon and reflected on our choice to live a vowed life in community, each of the sisters shared her response, contributing in her own way to this "memoir of many voices."

Why did you choose to enter a vowed life?

"I felt a change in the direction of my life at an early age. I hadn't thought of becoming a sister. I had other plans. The calling from God was unmistakable; I couldn't ignore it. But I had to move on it, I had to intentionally make the choice. That's the mystery."

"What began as a gesture of curiosity ended in a firm commitment to a counter-cultural life. I responded to a simple invitation to view a film on religious life and hang out with other girls my age at a convent across town. As a result of that afternoon, my calling somehow turned from curiosity to interest, leading to a time of investigation and ended with crossing the United States to find the community of God's choice for me!"

"My life was going on, but in no particular direction. I felt happy, but unclear as to what my future would be. When I realized I had a calling to a vowed life, I knew I could not do it on my own. That's where faith came in. I had a total need for God to help me live this life. So, I turned it over to Him with the belief that He would help me. In return, I promised God I would do my best."

What does it mean to live a vowed life?

"To me it means that I have vows to live up to daily. And I live in community with others who do as well. I enjoy the schedule of the liturgical life."

"Benedictines follow the Rule of St. Benedict – obedience, stability, and fidelity to the monastic way of life (previously called *Conversatio morum,* Conversion of life). These vows also include poverty and chastity."

Sisters Andrine and Andriette Schommer, Anne Boeckers, and Eleanor Wartman celebrating their 60th Jubilee

"We empathize with those in need of an ear and heart. It is a blessing to have time to read and pray, to give and take with community – financially, lovingly, socially, and prayerfully."

Sisters Mary, Paula, Lucia, and Karen playing Rummikub after dinner

"As a Benedictine we live in community and have genuine care and respect for one another. We support one another in the work we do, we pray with others; we pray and work together."

"This life is calm and peaceful. It gives you a feeling that someone special is helping you see the beauty in people and nature."

"I am learning each day what it means to 'prefer nothing whatsoever to Christ'" (RB 72:11).

What is your response to the three vows of Obedience, Stability, and Fidelity to the Monastic Way of Life?

"The *locus* of community may be within a monastery, or a parish, or even a temporary apartment, but essentially it is the relationships sustained among the vowed religious that generate stability and a sense of home."

"No matter what is happening in today's world, we need to remain a place of prayer and a stable community. Our achievements mean more than numbers and buildings."

Community Prayer is at the center of Monastic Life

"Obedience to our elected prioress is not problematic; we are not an autocratic community. 'I need a leaning,' one of our leaders used to request in search of consensus. I have been able to find my calling as I join in discernment with my prioress and the other sisters."

"We try to take responsibility for our talents. Benedictines respond to local needs as teachers, nurses, parish liturgists, writers, musicians, counsellors, leaders, artists, and more. Our various ministries allow us to take the Benedictine values outside the monastery and then return for support and stability."

"In becoming a sister, you open yourself to a lifetime of learning what it means to dedicate your life to God. As you bear witness to life as a Benedictine sister, you live in community. It is truly a family way of life. There are good times

It truly is a family way of life!

and challenging times along the way as I live my life to the fullest."

How do you see the Benedictine sisters of St. Paul's Monastery living and serving in today's society?

"I have a strong sense that to be able to fully live and serve today requires a good sense of humor, among other traits. In many ways, I feel my life is sort of a comedy of errors. I told the Lord, 'This is what you get.' But I have come to realize that whatever the Lord asks of me is all right . . . even the funny!"

Sisters Sharon Schiller (50th Jubilee) and Marie Fujan (60th Jubilee)

"In today's society, I believe we serve as an oasis of peace. St. Paul's Monastery is a place of safety, quiet, and rest. Here, everyone is accepted for who they are. There's dignity in that. Some people never feel that sense of worth until they come here. I have seen people cry when they are blessed with the gift of acceptance. Their self-image is raised. We treat each person who comes here with dignity."

"We stand as a quiet presence in the world. We focus on what we can give and do for others. It's how we live. There are abundant blessings in common, everyday life."

"At a younger age, I never wanted to be a sister, but I was raised to listen to God and to give everything to Him. I made a delayed choice as I came to realize there are more important things in life than what is valued in the world. It is true that we live simply with little need for the material, but we have our 'wealth' in the life we've chosen."

"Most people find their true vocation if they're lucky. Whether it's a life partnered in marriage, a single life, or a life vowed to Christ, our vocation is how we choose to dedicate our lives. Simply put, Benedictine sisters live vowed lives in community, following the Rule of Benedict, and we don't put anything before God."

"We must look for new layers of meaning in the world today. This 75th anniversary is a time to celebrate what we as sisters have accomplished, despite any hardships we have suffered."

Sisters on the plaza near St. Benedict

Chapter 7 – Former Members:
A Temporary Call

Louise Inhofer, OSB

As in a marriage, there are no simple answers to the question of why someone leaves a religious community. The reason someone comes to religious life is not always why they stay. Nor does one walk down the aisle on the day of profession with the intention to leave. A vowed commitment involves a daily "yes" to God. However, sometimes women hear a different call or seek a dispensation from their vows for individual reasons. And for those who do choose a different path, each day still offers opportunities to respond to God's call.

I never sought to be unique in any way, but I realize that today I am the only member of this community to have lived three phases as a Benedictine: a professed member, a laywoman, and now a professed member again.

I came to St. Paul's Priory on September 7, 1948, right after high school. When I became a novice, I was given the name Sister Louise. After studying at the Diocesan Teachers College and St. Catherine's College, I earned a degree in Elementary Education, teaching children in grades two through eight for nineteen years. Since many of the schools did not have a library, I tried to establish one, but organization was challenging. I loved the well-organized library at St. Anne's! In 1968 I received permission to pursue a degree as a librarian, so I applied to Western Michigan University in Kalamazoo, Michigan, where I earned an M.A. in Library Science. I enjoyed working as a full-time librarian in several schools.

The second part of my Benedictine life began when I left the monastery to live as a lay woman. The beginning of this thirty-year period was particularly challenging since I was on my own for the first time in my life. Finding housing, jobs (even losing one), managing finances, cooking, and shopping became daily challenges. But during this time, thankfully, I was also able to take care of my parents until their deaths. I made new friends, joined a book club and coffee club, and enjoyed square dancing, line dancing (even being in a performing group), and tap dancing. Life was good. But despite all this socializing, I was still living like a Benedictine but without vows, longing for what I had experienced in community, for what I was missing. In 2010 I became an Oblate, experienced the sisters' retreat, and was encouraged to inquire about the possibility of returning. It was something the Rule of Benedict allowed. My wish was granted, and I returned to the monastery soon after.

I am now living part three of my Benedictine life and loving it. When I first stepped into the new monastery I felt right at home and knew that God was calling me to live here. It was with joy that I disposed of the contents of my apartment, giving much of it to friends and family. Many items are here in the monastery, and it is nice to see them being used by so many sisters. The hardest part was having to give up my cat, Ashley. Living at home again with the sisters, especially my sister, Sister Mary Claire, there is always someone to say 'good morning' to, share a meal with, grow with, and especially pray with. Praying alone has its merits, (although Ashley had 'prayed' along too) but being able to pray with the community is one of God's many gifts and full of blessings. I am the monastic librarian and am right at home in the library which keeps me busy, while also sharing in our broader community life of prayer and work.

Part four in my Benedictine journey is unknown to me, but I know God will provide.

Sister Louise in the monastic library at St. Paul's Monastery

Following are some thoughts expressed by other women who had felt called to St. Paul's Monastery, but later chose a new path in their life journey:

"I could never repay you, dear sisters, for all I experienced in community: prayer, work duties, recreation, and silence."

Thanks for helping me become the person I am today.

Former members Theresa McPartlin, Pat Jones, and Jane Wagemaker return to the monastery to thank the sisters

"I was able to provide service in teaching and social work with the fine education I was given. I have used these skills to serve in all my employment because making a difference has been my focus, not making the highest salary."

I came because of God's call, and I left because He was redirecting me.

"Thanks for helping me become the person I am today."

"I believed, and still do, that God called me to the monastery, and then out of it, because of who I am and the things I needed to experience, heal, and accomplish. My life was one of searching for God and healing."

"Monastic life has not failed me, or I it. I came because of God's call, and I left because He was redirecting me. I have a foundation for my life and courage I didn't have when I entered. I will continue to do His work."

"I will always think of the sisters of St. Paul's Monastery as my family. I appreciate their prayers and sincere hospitality. Whenever I come through the door, I still feel very much a part of the community."

Sister Eleanor Wartman with a former member Mary Ann Carr

"Your monastery is a center of prayer and peace in Maplewood. It is a holding point for peace in the world, an anchor."

Chapter 8 – Benedictine Associates: A New Form of Benedictine Community

Benedictine Associates

A number of women who were already affiliated with the monastery as volunteers and/or oblates had expressed a desire for an even closer relationship with the Sisters of St. Paul's Monastery. Some of these women had considered the call to religious life; others desired an affiliation with the sisters and their good works while living a lay life. Conversations arose around the idea of alternative forms of association with the vowed sisters.

In the Fall of 2010, the Sisters of St. Paul's Monastery decided to invite a number of these laywomen to join them in small groups to discuss and research this possibility. Together with several sisters and under the facilitation of Oblate Mary Dickinson, these women helped to lay the groundwork for the foundation of a new vocational choice for single, Catholic women, "Benedictine Associate." Each Benedictine associate will share in the life, prayers, and services of the sisters and receive continued enrichment in Benedictine values and the Benedictine way of life. Each Benedictine associate is given the option to make a commitment to this way of life on a yearly basis. On March 21, 2014, a new ministry was launched with a formal commitment ceremony, at which time Linda Anderson and Mary Lou Kozmik became the charter associates. Over the past eight years, seven women have made their commitment.

Sister Karen Sames with Benedictine Associates Mary Lou Kozmik, Linda Anderson, Rebekah Taylor, Patricia Swanke, and Sister Catherine Nehotte.

The Associate Committee, comprised of laywomen, associates, and sisters, oversees the administration of this ministry. The committee ensures an appropriate formation schedule is maintained, consisting of at least two sessions each year, as well as confirming that associates are honoring their commitment to the sisters. Their ministry of service is tailored to the needs of the community and paired with the desires and skills of each woman. Benedictine associates are welcome to lead daily prayers, assist at Eucharist, prepare Vigil reflections, participate in and lead monastery committees, help in the Healthcare Center, aid in various housekeeping tasks as well as assist with community events, or offer hospitality to the Benedictine Center guests. At a special yearly service, each associate is offered the opportunity to renew her commitment.

Sister Agnes Trombley, the community representative on the initial committee, felt the associate ministry closed a gap for single, Catholic women, filling the space between vowed religious life on the one hand, and the oblate ministry available to married or single Christian men and women on the other. She marveled at the bond that quickly formed among the associates as well as between associates and sisters. Sister Paula participated in laying the foundation for this ministry and strongly supported it in the first years of its inception. She notes, "Associates came with innovative ideas and energy to learn about the Benedictine traditions and history. I was delighted to provide some of their formation classes. They came well prepared with questions from their readings and often offered creative ideas. They were especially interested in serving the sisters in health care and the community liturgy. I see enormous potential for the future." Sister Karen Sames, the current community representative on the committee, feels that she has been blessed to collaborate with these wonderful women: "We took a long time to lay a solid foundation for this ministry. During the years of the pandemic we met virtually every month, often sharing our hopes, concerns, and values."

This relatively new associate ministry continues to evolve and touch the lives of all involved in both spiritual and temporal ways. From the community's perspective, the sisters feel supported by these laywomen who also have a deep love for Christ and who find Benedictine spirituality to be a powerful way to live gospel values.

"The Benedictine Associates have blessed my life in many ways," said Sister Karen. "I have been challenged and inspired through our shared articles, conferences, retreats, and social gatherings. Their assistance in the monastery ministries and tasks is invaluable. The COVID-19 pandemic was challenging, and we had to be resourceful with how we stayed connected. The bond that was already in place between the associates and sisters enabled a life-giving respite from the isolation caused by the pandemic. We have shared more deeply because of the relationship we have formed and the way in which we have connected."

Certainly, the lives of these women who have committed to live as associates have changed through this ministry. Developing a personal prayer life, caring compassionately for the sisters, and participating in ministries have enriched and transformed them. To capture their experience in their own words:

"The Associate Ministry allows me to see and experience Benedictine spirituality in the day-to-day lives of the sisters, which draws me closer to God by supplying the support I need to live it in my daily life. In particular, the practice of integrating prayer and work (Ora et Labora) in all things has brought me closer to God. Benedictine living has provided balance, stability and 'right priorities' in my overall life. I have grown in so many ways by hearing the personal stories of the sisters and the other associates and seeing the beautiful souls they are. They have become my other family." (Associate Linda Anderson, 9 years)

"The monastery has been a spiritual home where I feel most welcome. Being associated with the sisters fills my longing to share with like-minded people. Joining the sisters in singing the psalms at the Liturgy of the Hours fills me with joy. The memory of that joy sometimes lingers and wells up in my heart other hours of the day when I'm doing ordinary tasks. I feel enriched when leading Morning or Evening Praise at the Monastery and the sisters have told me that they welcome and appreciate my participation. When I volunteer, I am blessed! New spiritual doors have opened for me since I met these sisters." (Associate Mary Lou Kozmik, 9 years)

"As a Benedictine Associate, I have found fellowship and purpose in the company of these women. In our increasingly secular culture, it is not always easy to find companions who are devoted to Christ and the Church. Neither is it easy to find friendships formed upon shared values that go beyond the superficial. Whether we are praying together in Chapel, sitting around the campfire, serving others, studying the Rule of Benedict, giggling over a game of dominoes, or mourning the loss of someone we love, we are aware of the precious gift of our bond." (Associate Rebekah Taylor, 3 years)

"The Associate Ministry has accelerated my understanding of Benedictine spirituality, which is key to helping me more consistently live out gospel values. I have come to a deeper understanding of what is meant by 'listening with the ear of one's heart.' I recognize the importance of prayer, quiet, and solitude in deepening my connection with Christ and realizing God's plan for my life. I have come to love the other associates and sisters who have become an integral part of my life." (Associate Pat Swanke, 1 year)

Thirteen years ago, the first Associate Committee sought and listened for guidance from the Holy Spirit in their administration of this new ministry. This was when Sister Agnes pointed out that perhaps the Spirit will take St. Paul's Monastery's Benedictine community and this ministry in a new direction. Today, we also look to the future: the annual commitment renewal that often occurs on the Feast of St. Benedict helps the associate and the community stay in the moment even as we continue to engage in ongoing discernment. As Sister Paula remarked years ago, "I see exciting potential for the future."

Perhaps the Holy Spirit will take our Benedictine community in a new direction.

Chapter 9 – Oblates: Sharing the Benedictine *Charism*

Mary Lou Dummer, OSB

O ur 75th anniversary also marks the 43rd year of the Oblate Community of St. Paul's Monastery numbering approximately two hundred — men and women, married and single, young and senior, ecclesial ministers and laity, of various Christian faiths — who have discovered that the guidelines for Christian living written by St. Benedict over 1500 years ago are a gift today.

Sister Mary Lou opens the 2019 Oblate Retreat

Like monastic women and men, oblates do not see their lives as a static state of perfection, but as a journey of coming to recognize human weakness and then depend on God's mercy to help them grow as understanding and compassionate persons. Each one — whether a Methodist minister (our first oblate in 1980), or a Catholic woman, or a Lutheran Minnesota grandfather — lives the Gospel life within their own faith tradition, cherishing their distinct culture, continuing their occupation, caring for their families, and enjoying their blessings. In short, in their effort to balance their lives with prayer, work, and leisure, oblates live their ordinary lives in an extraordinary way. Having made a formal commitment, they regard themselves as "co-holders of the Benedictine tradition."

Integrating Benedictine values into their lives, they become Christ's presence in their families, church, cities, towns, neighborhoods, and workplaces. Indeed, the difference they make in their world helps to change the whole world. They are known to have engaged in outreach ministry with Hmong youth, senior citizens, a Guatemalan family, the Dorothy Day canonization effort, and have participated in both regional and national oblate conferences. With St. Paul's Monastery as a spiritual home, oblates offer their various services as readers, prayer leaders, musicians, hospitality ministers, drivers, even bakers and occasional furniture movers. This unique relationship with the Sisters of St. Paul's Monastery offers a rich opportunity for deep spiritual growth, for the stability of community, and for service to the sisters and to the world.

Kathy Holt, Lorraine Schwarzrock, Nancy Cicero and Sister Karen

To prepare to practice this "good zeal to which our Holy Father Benedict has called us" (RB 72), the oblates spend close to a year in formation, with the sisters sharing their spiritual journey as they meet monthly to learn the Rule of Benedict and practice Benedictine values: awareness of God, hospitality, community, listening, justice, the dignity of work (Ora et Labora), moderation, peace, respect for persons, and stewardship. They also pray with the sisters or in small groups with one another online or in person, practicing the Liturgy of the Hours, *Lectio Divina*, and centering prayer. After a retreat Day of Discernment, each candidate, with the support of his or her sister sponsor, creates a formation document in response to the question, "How does following the Rule of St. Benedict by living the life of an Oblate enhance my relationship with Christ, this community, and others?"

Today, many oblates recognize that as the sisters age, the oblates themselves will not only serve alongside the sisters but also carry the legacy of the sisters' ministry forward. Oblate Travis Salisbury remarks, "It is vital that oblates will need to assume more responsibility for ongoing formation as oblate inquirers and candidates choose this way of life." And indeed, a recently established Advisory Committee comprised solely of oblates has created a number of optional, small interest groups that meet either in person or online to fortify community. The topics include centering prayer, creative writing, the beauty of nature, listening to God, walking, and a book discussion.

Oblate group of 2019: Marcia Bailey, Paula Hurley, Jim Hansen,
Benjamin Wagner, Steve Ellison, Jeff Dols, Emily Broeffle

In their own words of praise:

"I value personal retreats at the monastery, praying the Liturgy of the Hours with the sisters and alone, experiencing the silence and peace." (Active Oblate)

"We must reach beyond the monastery walls, embrace the Rule of Benedict, and continue to apply its wisdom to our daily lives for the next 75 years! We rejoice in the gift that is and has been, the Sisters of St. Paul's Monastery." (Travis Salisbury, Oblate 2015, Director of Mission Advancement)

"Being an oblate is not an addition to my life; it is a stream unto itself, guiding, provoking, and leading me deeper into the life of Christ and Christ's community." (Gwen Odney, Episcopal Faith Tradition, Oblate 2016)

"Volunteering at the former Monastery (now Harriet Tubman Center East) allows me to meet people at the door, welcoming them and offering stable housing for many in desperate situations." (An Oblate Porter)

"The Monastery enfolds us in the stability of perseverance, the listening of obedience, and the conversation of transformation." (Active Oblate)

Chapter 10 – Benedictine Center:
A Sacred Threshold for the Laity
by Jeff Dols, Oblate

In conjunction with the 75th anniversary of St. Paul's Monastery, the Benedictine Center celebrates its 40th year. Since 1983, the Center has been an enduring ministry, offering an opportunity for a time away within a monastic environment to discover the presence of God in ourselves, in other persons, and in the world around us. Both a sacred threshold and an outreach of the Monastery, the Center offers monastic space and support for contemplation.

Sister Veronica Novotny, its first director, was a visionary who in the 1980s was already looking to the next century to see what was needed. Having taught in the parishes, she saw the spiritual hunger of the laity and recognized that they needed to experience what is core to monastic life: prayer, reflective reading, and discerning apostolic work. Thus, she explored the possibility of creating a spirituality center that would provide divine nourishment to a frenetic world while honoring the rhythm of monastic life. Asserting that Benedictines have been recognized for their relevance during each era of history, she claimed that the Center "would meet the changing needs of our world for years to come, be a service to our Church, and a strong testimony to Benedict's instruction: 'Let all guests who arrive be received as Christ'" (RB 53:1).

"The Benedictine Center was created for our own community as well," says Sister Virginia Matter. "Veronica knew that the

Benedictine Rule has so many practical ideas for living together peacefully. We welcome seekers to walk with Benedictines as pilgrims have for centuries, sharing what is learned and lived together." The sisters themselves were encouraged to seek spiritual direction as well as be trained as spiritual directors, for Sister Veronica believed that "spiritual renewal is important for monastics and non-monastics alike."

After a feasibility committee, pilot programs, and community approval, on August 15, 1983, the retreat center was officially approved by the Monastic Council. It offered hospitality, spiritual direction, meditation, Catholic liturgy, psychotherapy, and individual or group retreats with particular attention to women, family life, and single parenting. It remains the only retreat center in the Twin Cities yoked with a living monastic community. This unusual feature initially

Sister Veronica Novotny,
founder of the Benedictine Center

called for a delicate balance: the sisters cherished their private cloistered space separate from the guest rooms while simultaneously participating in harmony with the visitors in chapel, refectory, art gallery, and meeting rooms. Over the years the shared rhythms of monastic life relaxed somewhat to include thousands of lay and clerical retreatants. Sister Duane Moes, prioress at the time, notes that "it was difficult to get off the ground but look how it's grown. So, it's having a ripple-out effect in families and the larger community. Thousands have been touched."

With Sister Virginia and Sister Mary White as staff, contemplative prayer and meditation as presented by Father Thomas Keating, O.C.S.O. and other Benedictines became the foundational approach. Today innovative methods of retreat ministry such as practicing Lectio Divina with couples, writing, poetry, pottery, visual arts, and even pilgrimages acknowledge changing times and guests. "Our constant call is to be a place of respite, a home to be refreshed, a setting in which people feel nurtured and at peace. More and more people are coming for quiet time," Sister Virginia observes. "They tell us 'I just need space' or 'I need time by myself to think and be quiet.' The world keeps pushing. There is a hunger out there."

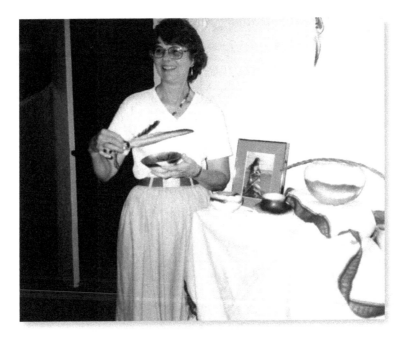

Sister Virginia Matter in pottery studio, 1983

Even as retreatants are able to rest in quiet, they are also invited to participate in either of two "schools for the Lord's service" ("Prologue" RB) – a School of Lectio Divina about learning how to pray and a School of Discernment about prayerful decision-making. As Sister Mary White reminds us, "The contemplative meditation of a Benedictine is meant to move one toward action."

By 2013, the Center had held 2,000 guests every year and offered one hundred retreats, workshops, and prayer sessions for individuals as well as groups. Twenty-first century strategic planning sessions reaffirmed the ministry, now housed in the new monastery, as a viable extension of the monastic community with a focus on biblical, liturgical spirituality based on Benedictine history and tradition, supported by the presence of a stable monastic community. A website, a brochure, the publication *Listen,* an arts and spirituality program, partnership with St. John's University, and even pilgrimages to Wales and Korea — all have ensued. Recently a survey of guests (parishioners, ministers, pastors, spiritual directors, and teachers) identified key elements they believe people need to thrive spiritually:

"I need time by myself to think and be quiet."

- Times of silence and solitude
- A community that welcomes all people wherever they are on their spiritual journey, and spiritual practices that open them up to hear God's voice
- Cultivating a sense of joy and gratitude
- Authenticity: to be true and real in one's relationships with God, with others, and with one's own spiritual practices
- To appreciate one's own humanity and the humanity of others through a heart of compassion and love
- Spiritual companions, both one-on-one and in groups, who can listen as we go deeper.

One "spiritual companion" unique to the Benedictine monastic world is the porter. Long-time Benedictine Center Director, Sam Rahberg and Associate Director Kiely Todd Roska identified the importance of the Benedictine value of hospitality through the role of porter:

"In the Rule, St. Benedict commends the role of the porter, the person stationed at the front door and responsible for greeting visitors to the Monastery. Whenever a visitor showed up, the porter was supposed to shout, 'Thanks be to God!' or 'Your blessing please!' (RB 66). The porter embodied the commitment to greet everyone as Christ, engaging every new arrival as a person carrying a blessing.

"Members of the Benedictine Center staff, and team of volunteers often get to practice the role of 'porter' at the Monastery, being entrusted with the task of greeting every guest with the 'warmth of love.' We welcome people in whatever state they arrive for a time of retreat. Some people arrive full of gratitude and joy, brimming with a story they simply must share. Others come primed for learning, ready to join in conversation about how they might live out Benedictine values in their daily lives in meaningful ways. Some come seeking beauty, taking in the latest art exhibit. Still others arrive tired, weary, or worn down from life's pressures.

"However, all guests are seeking renewal for their journey. The first sign they have come to the right place is the way the porter greets them with arms and heart wide open. At St. Paul's Monastery, pilgrims find porters ready to listen for what a person really needs, and eager to offer the gifts the sisters share: quiet, nourishment, rest, companions in prayer.

"The privilege of the porter is to live on the edge of expectancy. The next guest to arrive is sure to bring a blessing. That guest might very well be reading this article now and soon to arrive for a workshop, retreat, or an opportunity to prayer.

The next guest to arrive is sure to bring a blessing!

Know that a team of porters is eagerly and warmly awaiting your arrival" ("The Porter," September 2019).

All are welcomed by Oblate Travis Salisbury

Closed for 18 months because of the COVID-19 pandemic, the Benedictine Center reopened in September of 2021 to once more welcome guests. In a spirit of hope, the Center is reimaging how to continue as a School of the Lord's Service, sharing Benedictine values as an enduring legacy of St. Paul's Monastery.

In his last *Listen* publication column in January 2020, Sam Rahberg provided this timeless call to action:

"I hear an urgency in the *Rule* that we dare not disregard. Imagine Benedict himself, standing today at the door of St. Paul's Monastery, as we all gather around. We hear him proclaim the words from the Prologue to the *Rule*:

> *Listen carefully, my children!*
> *Is there anyone who yearns for life?*

At one time, his invitation might have been more clearly directed to those who wanted to become monks. Today, however, Benedict's rousing charge speaks to many, many more. People drawn to Benedictine spirituality sense his charge to 'get up at long last' as fueled by prayer and a conviction that refuses to let them carry on with life as usual. Some expectancy brought them to the front door of a monastery. Some movement of the Spirit opened wide the ear of their hearts to carry Benedictine values into the world of our communities, families, and workplaces" ("Moving Benedictine Values into the World").

Benedictine Center guests

Looking to the Future

Catherine Nehotte, OSB Prioress

The past 25 years have gone by quickly. As I read this anniversary book, I am reminded of the many things that have taken place, our many accomplishments, and our challenges. My heart is hopeful as I look towards our centennial anniversary with eager anticipation. There will be changes; however, with the grace of God we will find the future to which God is calling us.

I pray that women today who are being called by God to a life of community and service will take time to discern the possibility of a vowed religious life. Moreover, being a single Catholic woman, Benedictine Associate, or an Oblate (male or female, single or married, from all faiths) are other ways to associate with us in living Benedictine values while residing in your own home and neighborhood.

Benedict was a layman living in the midst of a violent world, much like our own.

We are also blessed to have many lay people sharing our mission as employees or volunteers, each with unique and bountiful gifts. While some have served in key leadership roles, all share their time, talent, and resources which have enhanced what this community provides through our ministries. Their presence has enriched our community and given us a unique perspective of a society that I believe is crying out for spirituality.

God is a God of surprises! As we ponder ways to preserve our legacy, God brings us what we need to remain a center of contemplation in a busy suburb. Today, our mission is to offer hospitality, stability, community, prayer, and peace to all — the peace of which St. Benedict speaks. Benedict was a layman living in the midst of a violent world, much like our own. Benedict continues to invite us to "listen with the ear of the heart" and welcome each person as Christ, reverence all things as the vessels of the altar, and preserve the gifts of nature.

God is a God of surprises!

We cannot be sure what the next 25 years will hold. But we do know that we will continue to listen to God as did our founder Benedict, Mother Benedicta Riepp who centuries later crossed the ocean to found a Benedictine Motherhouse in America, and to our own 178 charter sisters who left St. Benedict's Convent in St. Joseph, Minnesota in 1948 to begin this community in St. Paul. Today, we, the Sisters of St. Benedict of St. Paul's Monastery welcome the future to which God is calling us as we look to our centennial year and beyond.

"That in all things, God may be glorified" (1 Peter 4:11)

Lucia Schwickerath, OSB

Writing the 75th anniversary history of our community was a challenging assignment in the journey of my life. My Bachelor of Music degree and Master's degree in Liturgy and Music provided little guidance on how to research or write the history of a community. However, more than 60 years of lived experience in community as liturgist, novice director, or prioress often placed me at the heart of the community. With Pope Francis, I concur that the "recounting of our history is essential for preserving our identity, for strengthening our unity as a family and our common sense of belonging. More than an exercise in archaeology or the cultivation of mere nostalgia, it calls for following in the footsteps of past generations in order to grasp the high ideals, and the vision and values which inspired them, beginning with the founders and foundresses and the first communities. In this way we come to see how the charism has been lived over the years, the creativity it has sparked, the difficulties it encountered and the concrete ways those difficulties were surmounted. To tell our story is to praise God and to thank him for all his gifts" (Pope Francis "Aims of the Year of consecrated Life" I, 1).

Compiling this book brought me to a deeper awareness of each sister as a gift, gave me a greater respect for authors and editors, and made me more skilled in interviewing, writing, and collaborating; however, and most significantly, it deepened my faith in the ever-present God who co-created this book and companioned me daily.

First, I want to publicly thank Sister Catherine Nehotte, Prioress, who placed her confidence in me to coordinate the production of this book and the sisters of St. Paul's Monastery for their undaunted trust and complete cooperation. This group of vowed women served as my main support by their inspiration, affirmation, and encouragement. They have become my family and I am profoundly grateful for each of them. In addition, I appreciated the willingness of numerous community friends, relatives, and acquaintances who helped, each in their own way.

Next, as you can imagine, I could not have told the stories that unfolded during the past 25 years alone. Thank you to the five prioresses who shared their perception of God's grace to community during their time of leadership, providing much of the content. Thank you to other contributors: Sister Mary Lou Dummer, Jeff Dols, Sister Louise Inhofer, and all who shared their life experiences in personal witness for our edification.

"So that in all things God may be glorified!"

Finally, I am especially grateful to my publishing team: Sheila Bartle, (Assistant Editor) friend of the Benedictines, retired professor, author, editor, and writing coach who spent endless hours editing; Oblate Jeff Dols, (Publishing Coordinator) author, retired Benedictine Center Director and long-time monastery volunteer who coordinated the final steps of this publication; and Jean Martens, (Manuscript Editor) a personal friend and previous coworker who shared her writing and organizational skills to position the book content to allow you greater reading pleasure and encouraged me continually during production. Without their help, I could not have produced this book and so it would have forever remained an unrealized dream. Because of the efforts of this team and the assistance of so many along the way, this book has become a reality "so that in all things God may be glorified!"

St. Paul's Monastery: Home of the Sisters of St. Benedict of St. Paul, Minnesota

References

Benedict of Nursia. *Benedict's Rule: A translation and Commentary.* Edited by Terrence G. Kardong. Collegeville, Minnesota: The Liturgical Press, 1981.

CICLSAL (Congregation for Institutes of Apostolic Life and Societies of Apostolic Life). *Apostolic Visitation of Institutes of Women Religious in the United States of America Final Report* (September 8, 2014).

Francis, His Holiness Pope. *Apostolic Letter to all Consecrated People on the occasion of the Year of all Consecrated Life.* (November 21, 2014). https://www.vatican.va/content/francesco/en/apost_letters/documents/papa-francesco_lettera- ap_20141121_lettera-consacrati.html.

Jurisich, Christine. *Retreat, Reflect, Renew: A Sacred Journal for a More Peaceful You.* Google: 2015

Rahberg, Sam. "Moving Benedictine Values into the World." *Listen* (January 2020).

Rahberg, Sam and Kiely Todd Roska. "The Porter: At the threshold of Hospitality." *Listen* (September 2019).

"Sister Carol Rennie Thrives on Teaching the Art of Teaching." *The Quarterly II,* no. 1 (September 1988).

Warner, Steven C. *Wake the World with Dawning Joy.* Notre Dame, Indiana: ASCAP, 2014.

"Wherever You Go." The Benedictine Foundation of the State of Vermont. (1972). www.westonpriory.org

Artist Michael Pilla

CPSIA information can be obtained
at www.ICGtesting.com
Printed in the USA
JSHW022318011222
34218JS00002B/7